LEVEL HEADERS

Love
BEING
YOU!

written by
Beth Cox & Natalie Costa

illustrated by
Vicky Barker

With thanks to the Inclusive Minds Inclusion Ambassadors for providing useful insights as this title was developed

www.bsmall.co.uk

Published by b small publishing ltd. www.bsmall.co.uk © b small publishing ltd. 2021 • 1 2 3 4 5 • ISBN 978-1-912909-94-0
Publisher: Sam Hutchinson   Editorial: Sam Hutchinson   Design and Art direction: Vicky Barker   Printed in China by WKT Co. Ltd.
All rights reserved. No reproduction, copy or transmission of this publication may be made without written permission. No part of this publication may be reproduced, stored in a retrieval system or transmitted in any form or by any means, electronic, mechanical, photocopying, recording or otherwise, without the prior permission of the publisher.
British Library Cataloguing-in-Publication Data. A catalogue record for this book is available from the British Library.

How this book works

This book is full of activities to help you explore who you are and how to value yourself. The activities all build on each other so are designed for you to work through in order, but you can skip some and go back if you want, or dip in and out if you'd rather — there are no rules.

Use the icons to find top tips, useful information, suggestions for taking it further and details of additional resources.

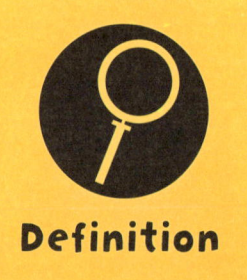

Useful info/fact

Take it further

Top tip

Make your own

Definition

Who are YOU?

What makes you who you are is a combination of what you do, how you think, how you treat people, what you look like, how you dress and how you express yourself. However, what you look like and how you dress are self-expression — it is how you feel about yourself, what you do and how you treat people that really matters.

Who you are on the inside is much more important than how you look on the outside. You may feel that you have flaws, but you are exactly the person you are supposed to be, facing exactly the challenges you are supposed to face. The most important thing is to be true to yourself, live your life well and look after the body that houses the person you are. Looking after your body is a huge part of this. It will help you feel better, give you more energy and even boost your brain power!

Contents

4-5	Your body can	20-21	Express yourself
6-7	You are made of stardust	22-23	Brain food
8-9	Everyone is unique	24-25	Food is fuel
10-11	'Normal' does not exist	26-27	Eating a rainbow
12-13	Look inside	28-29	Move your body
14-15	Belonging	30-31	Sleep is for superheroes!
16-17	Your body tells a story	32	Claiming your space
18-19	You are important		

Your body can

Your body is unique to you and can do amazing things. All bodies look different but having a body means that you are alive and have a place in the world.

Your heart beats 60 to 100 times a minute, pumping blood around your body to keep you alive.

Your brain sends signals to each part of your body telling it what to do.

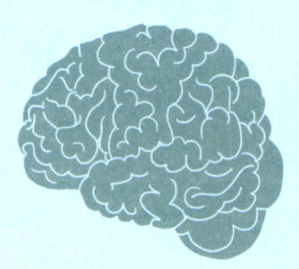

Your body digests food and, as the food passes through about seven metres of intestines, it takes all the nutrients you need to make your body healthy.

Your body also gives you messages. It tells you when it is hungry or thirsty or tired. It even tells you when you have not drunk enough fluid by making your wee very yellow.

Notice what other messages your body gives you throughout the day.

If an adult's blood vessels were all put in line, they would wrap around the world four times.

"Your body is the vehicle for your life. It gives you possibilities and choices, ambitions and power. It carries your dreams and allows you to try your best to make them come true."
- Nicola Morgan

My body can tell me when I'm feeling excited.

My body can use food to give me energy.

My body can dive to the bottom of the pool.

Draw yourself doing something you enjoy and write statements about the things that your body can do.

My body is amazing!

My body can
....
....
....
....

My body can
....
....
....
....

My body can
....
....
....
....

My body can
....
....
....
....

My body can
....
....
....
....

My body can
....
....
....
....

My body can
....
....
....
....

See what other amazing facts you can find out about your body.

You are made of stardust

Everything on Earth is made of stardust, including you! When a star dies, all the elements that made up that star combine in different ways to make gas, planets, water, more stars and eventually humans.

Stars are very far away and the light they give out takes a long time to reach us. Some of the stars we see in the sky no longer exist. But we can still see their impact, even when they are gone.

Much like the stars, we all shine in our own way. Remember that you are as unique and as awe-inspiring as a star!

Every few years your body is recreated. Your body is not one solid object but is in fact made up of 7 billion, billion, billion atoms all held together. Cells divide and grow and age and die — you have an entirely new outer layer of skin every year and your skeleton renews itself completely every 10 years.

"You couldn't be here if stars hadn't exploded, because the elements — the carbon, nitrogen, oxygen, iron ... were created in the nuclear furnaces of stars."
- Lawrence M. Krauss

1. On a clear night, go outside either into the garden, on a balcony or to the park with an adult. Lie down under the stars. Even if it's hard to see them, know they are still there.

Big Dipper

Lyra

Delphinus

2. Lie still for five minutes and think about how being under the sky and the stars makes you feel. Do you feel connected and part of something bigger? Or small in comparison?

3. Make some notes or draw how you feel lying under the stars.

4. In the same way the stars make you feel a certain way, think about how you want to make other people feel. What is it that you want to be known for?

Find out more about the constellations, or visit an online planetarium to see the stars.

Everyone is unique

No two people are the same — even identical twins are not exactly alike. If everyone were the same, life would be really boring! We are all more similar than different, but our differences are what make us who we are.

Knowing people who have other interests expands your world view and helps you to discover new things. They might introduce you to a new song, an unusual activity, a new language or even a new way of thinking about something.

👍 Human skin colour is mostly determined by the level of the pigment melanin that the body produces.

"What sets you apart can sometimes feel like a burden and it's not. And a lot of the time, it's what makes you great."
- Emma Stone

Why are we friends?

What is your favourite song?

What is your favourite colour?

What makes you excited?

What makes you feel calm?

Discover your similarities and differences by asking your friends these questions.

Add a piece of paper to your chart, if you want to continue writing down how you are similar to and different from your friends.

Me		

'Normal' does not exist

Books, television, adverts and the internet often show us certain types of people or ways of being. These people or ways of being become familiar and seem 'normal'. It is easy to start believing that this is how we should be too.

But normal does not really exist. Because what is 'normal' is different for everyone. What is normal for you might be unusual for someone else.

Despite what messages we receive, there is no one way to look, no one type of family, colour of skin or type of body that is more normal than another. The things that might not seem 'normal' to you are actually just things that you are not familiar with ... yet!

I live with my grandparents.

I live with my mums.

I have a bath before I go to bed.

I have a shower in the morning.

I get up early to go swimming on Saturday mornings.

I stay in my pyjamas and watch cartoons on Saturday mornings.

"Normal is not something to aspire to, it's something to get away from."
- Jodie Foster

What is your 'normal'?

Who do you live with?

What is your heritage?

Do you have any routines or rituals?

What traditions do you have?

How do you celebrate?

Share your normal with your friends and find out what is normal to them. You might be surprised by how they are different from you!

11

Look inside

Have you ever heard the phrase 'never judge a book by its cover'? People do this all the time! Your brain makes quick judgements about all of the information you receive every day. The world is complicated and your brain (and everybody else's!) needs to simplify things to cope.

The problem is, these quick judgements are often wrong. Have you ever thought something about someone and then, after getting to know them, you realise that you were completely wrong? Or perhaps you found out they were interested in something that you would never have guessed by looking at them. What we see when we look at someone only tells us part of the story.

What do you see first? Can you see something else? Once you see something one way, it is much harder to see it as something different.

1.
Draw or stick a picture of yourself here.

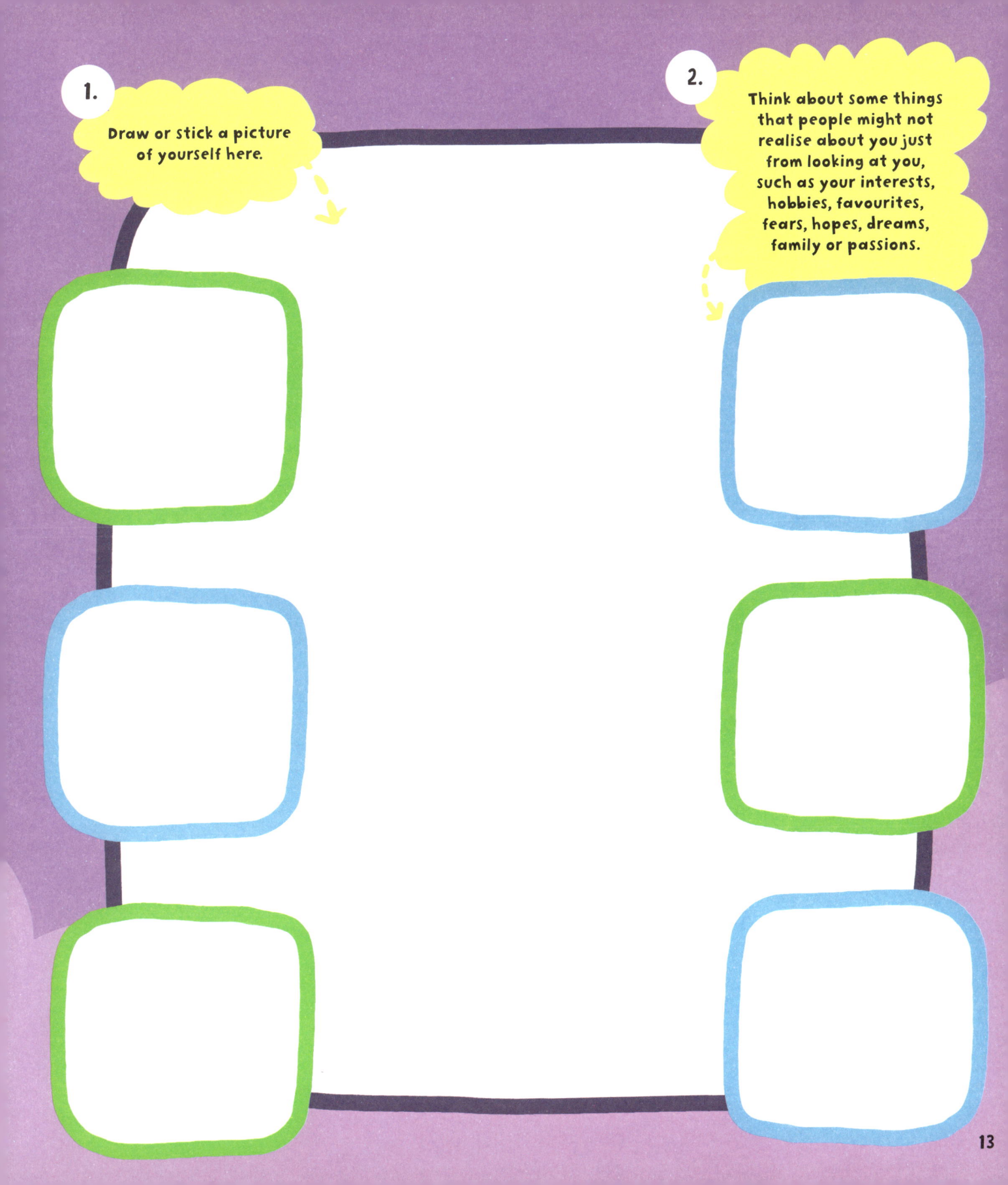

2.
Think about some things that people might not realise about you just from looking at you, such as your interests, hobbies, favourites, fears, hopes, dreams, family or passions.

Belonging

Belonging is not about fitting in with a group. It is about being who you truly are. Sometimes you can forget to be yourself, or try to hide parts of who you are in order to blend in. You will never really feel like you belong anywhere if you are not being yourself.

The first step to belonging is to accept who you are and not try to change what it is that makes you ... you! This may feel awkward at first and you might feel more out of place but you cannot feel like you belong without doing this. Start to look at how the real you is similar to others rather than different from them. There will be differences, but people are more alike than not.

"Always be a first-rate version of yourself, instead of a second rate version of somebody else." - Judy Garland

1. Draw or write the name of someone who you think is very different from you in each circle.

2. Start by writing why you think those people are different from you. Now think of at least three ways in which you are similar.

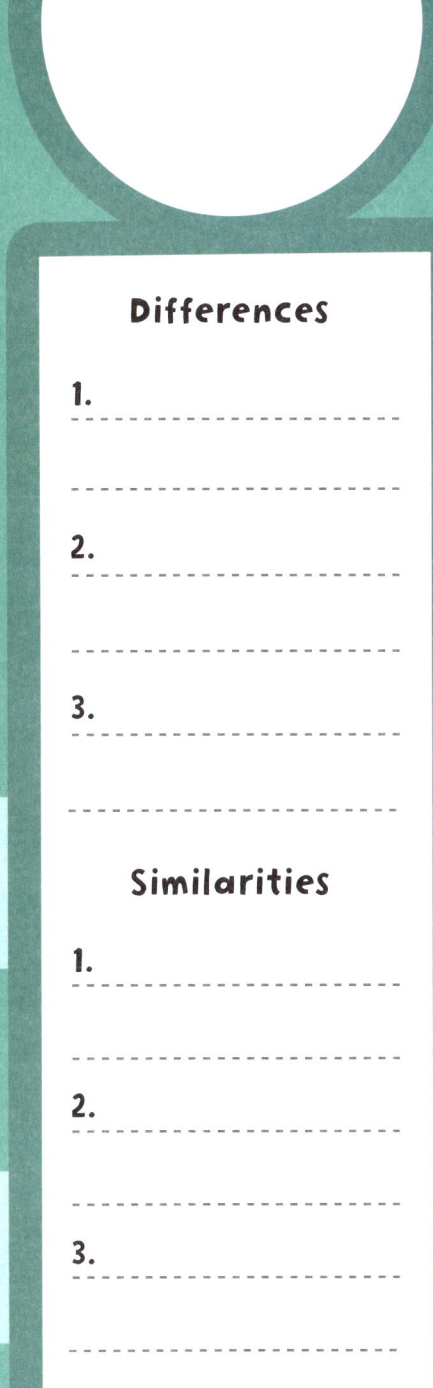

Differences

1. ....

....

2. ....

....

3. ....

....

Similarities

1. ....

....

2. ....

....

3. ....

....

Differences

1. ....

....

2. ....

....

3. ....

....

Similarities

1. ....

....

2. ....

....

3. ....

....

Differences

1. ....

....

2. ....

....

3. ....

....

Similarities

1. ....

....

2. ....

....

3. ....

....

Your body tells a story

Everyone's body tells a story. Whether it is DNA and genes telling a story about your heritage or a scar that reminds you of that time you fell off the swings. Although some things might make you feel self-conscious, it is important to remember that these things are part of what makes you who you are.

Rather than feeling self-conscious, celebrate the story of you! After all, it is a story that is unique and truly important.

I have blonde hair, which might be because of my Swedish heritage.

I wear an eye patch to help my other eye to get stronger.

My finger is a bit crooked because I broke it playing basketball.

"It is perfect to be imperfect because perfection is made up of many imperfections put together that make it perfect."
- Yasmin Ahmad

Tell the story of one of your features. You can use words or pictures ... or even both and make a comic strip.

If you are not sure where to start, talk to one of the important people in your life. Find inspiration by asking them about your heritage, your background and what has happened in your life. There might even be a story about something that happened when you were younger that you do not remember.

You are important

Everyone is important and every living person has value and purpose. When you start focusing on what you can do and how your actions affect other people, it is much easier to see how important you really are. Your physical body allows you to do all these things. Without your body, you would not exist and you would not be able to do those things that matter.

> "You are perfect. To think anything less is as pointless as a river thinking that it's got too many curves, or that it moves too slowly, or that its rapids are too rapid."
> - Jen Sincero

I looked after my cat.

I was helpful at home.

I tried hard in the play.

Each day, write down two things you like about yourself, or two things you have done, tried or achieved.

Try and write something different every day. You can look back at this list to remind yourself of what is great about you.

Monday
1. _____
_____
2. _____
_____

Tuesday
1. _____
_____
2. _____
_____

Wednesday
1. _____
_____
2. _____
_____

Thursday
1. _____
_____
2. _____
_____

Friday
1. _____
_____
2. _____
_____

Saturday
1. _____
_____
2. _____
_____

Sunday
1. _____
_____
2. _____
_____

- achievements
- acts of kindness
- effort
- thoughtful things you have done
- perseverance
- what a friend has said about you

If you want to keep this up for more than a week, get a small notebook to use as a journal.

19

Express yourself

Sometimes it is easy to express yourself, but other times it can feel really scary and you might worry about what others will think or say. It is not always easy to stand out from the crowd, but it is important to be true to what you like, how you feel, who you want to be and what you want to wear.

It can take courage to do this, but doing scary things is often when the best things happen. When you are confident in who you are, people will accept you for who you are. When you are able to be genuine, others will feel more comfortable around you.

One thing you might find when you are being true to yourself is that not everyone will like it. There could be different reasons for this, but remember this is okay. Not everyone likes chocolate but that does not mean that chocolate tastes horrible.

"To be yourself in a world that is constantly trying to make you something else is the greatest accomplishment."
- Ralph Waldo Emerson

Design a T-shirt that expresses who you are. It could be something you would love to wear or that tells people a bit about you, or how you feel inside.

If you enjoyed this, why not design an entire outfit?!

Brain food

Food gives you energy! But did you know that food powers your brain too?

Over half of our brain is made of fat. It is basically the consistency of jelly and it needs fats in order to work well. But not all fat is helpful for your brain or your body. A good way to decide if a fat is useful for your brain is to think about how natural it is. Nature is very clever at producing things that are healthy for our bodies. If a food has been processed and had lots of things added to it, then these fats might not be natural or helpful for your body or brain.

Circle the fatty foods that help your brain work well (remember these are the ones that are most natural).

nuts

avocados

butter

fruit yoghurt

cake

seeds

dark chocolate

crisps

fish

eggs

plain yoghurt

cheese

whole milk

sweets

Other brainpower foods include blueberries, bananas, oats, lentils, lemons, beetroot, coconut and sweet potato. Try some of these, if you haven't before.

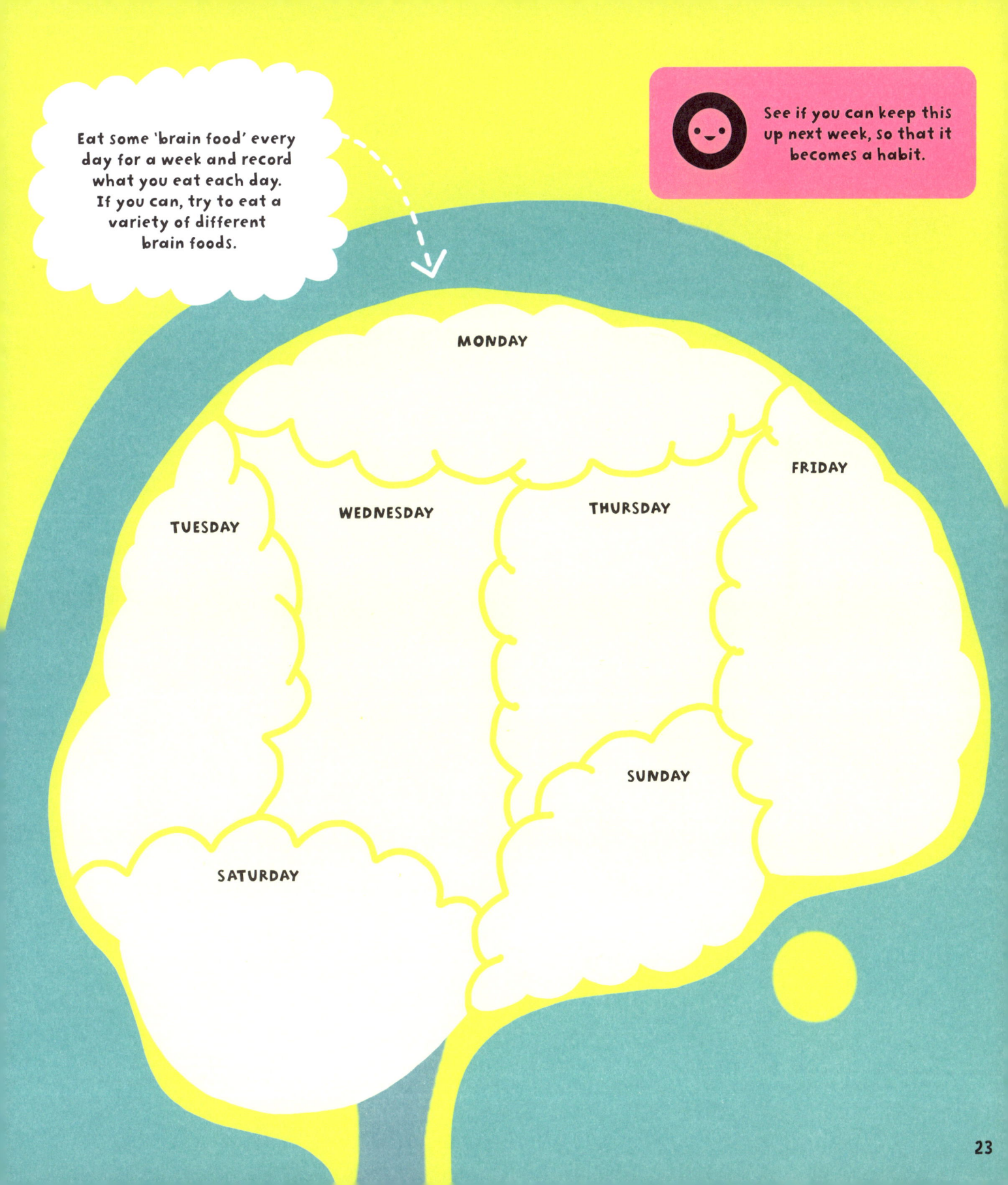

Eat some 'brain food' every day for a week and record what you eat each day. If you can, try to eat a variety of different brain foods.

See if you can keep this up next week, so that it becomes a habit.

MONDAY

TUESDAY

WEDNESDAY

THURSDAY

FRIDAY

SATURDAY

SUNDAY

Food is fuel

Food is fuel for your body but is also something to enjoy and savour. Eating well gives you more energy, helps you sleep better and assists your body in fighting off illness. Food is usually divided into food groups and eating from each group helps to keep your body in balance.

We are often told that some foods are good and some are bad. But food is just food. Some foods are better for your body than others but it is okay to eat absolutely any food as long as you have balance. Eating too much of one thing is not good for your body and might not help you feel full or give you the energy you need. If you only eat chips, your body will suffer ... but if will also suffer if you only eat carrots.

> Think about your favourite food or meal. Draw or write about it here. Does it contain something from all the food groups? What could you add to it to make it more balanced?

Ask yourself:

Have I already eaten something like this today?

What is this going to do for my body?

Foods that are not going to help your body are best kept as 'sometimes' foods, and those that will benefit your body can be 'everyday' foods.

Fruit and vegetables
(fresh, frozen, tinned)

Contain vitamins and minerals that are needed for changing food into energy and creating new cells. They also provide fibre that helps you digest your food and nutrients that help protect your body.

Whole grains
(pasta, bread, cereals, rice)

Keep you feeling full for longer, help your body to digest food and, as they move through your digestive system, remove chemicals that are bad for your body. They also help to control the chemical messengers that regulate mood and sleep.

Proteins
(meat, fish and beans)

Support the body to build muscle and help tissue to grow and to repair itself. Like whole grains, they help with mood and sleep and to keep you feeling full.

Fats and oils

Help to insulate the organs in your body to keep them safe. They also play a part in transporting some vitamins around the body. Fats and oils keep your joints healthy.

You do not have to include something from every food group in every meal, but aim for the food you eat to balance out over the day.

Sugars

Give your body energy quickly — but that can spike quickly and then go away, leaving you feeling more tired.

Milk and dairy

Provide vitamins and calcium to keep your bones and teeth strong.

Water

Makes up over half of your body. Drinking plenty of water keeps your body and your brain working well.

Eating a rainbow

Different foods provide different vitamins and minerals for your body. It would be impossible to try and remember which vitamins you get from which foods but luckily nature has given you a helping hand, once again.

Foods come in a range of natural colours. This is most obvious with fruit and vegetables. These colours give a clue about the vitamins and minerals the food provides. Eating foods that are a range of colours will help you get a wide range of vitamins. It can be harder than you think, but it is a good way to challenge yourself and to try new foods.

"... the food you eat should match the story you want to live, which means ... as colourful as possible, giving delight to the eyes ... maximising moments of happiness and pleasure."
- Deepak Chopra

Find as many food items as you can that are naturally each colour in this rainbow. See how many you can eat over a week. Can you try something new?

Red foods – help protect your heart and keep your body stable, keep your memory strong

Yellow/orange foods – protect you from illness, keep your joints healthy, fight toxins that are bad for your body

Green foods – keep bones and teeth strong, help fight off illness, help you see better, help you digest your food

Purple/blue foods – keep your eyes and tummy healthy, protect your body and fight off illness

White foods – keep your heart healthy, protect you from illness, help you digest your food

Make your own version of this rainbow and stick it up in your kitchen as a reminder of all the wonderful foods you can eat.

27

Move your body

When you move your body, you release endorphins. This is known as one of the 'happy hormones'. Keeping your body moving also helps your bones, joints and muscles to grow stronger — which in turn protects your body, keeps your heart healthy and helps you sleep better.

Everyone is different and you need to find an activity that works for you and your body — there are options for every single type of body. Some people prefer things fast and energetic, while others want something calm and gentle. Some like team sports, while others prefer to move on their own. If dancing is your preferred activity, you may want to do that in a group. Or you might be just as happy dancing alone, testing out your moves in private!

Take some time to find the type of movement that makes you happy.

1. Try some different types of activity, to see what you like best and what makes your body feel good. You may find only one thing that works well for you, or there might be lots of things. Write or draw in the box how each movement made you feel and what you discovered about what you like.

Team activities
(football, netball, basketball, hockey)

Solo activities
(swimming, yoga, running, cycling)

Calming activities
(yoga, swimming, climbing)

Lively activities
(dancing, playing at the park)

2. In here, write or draw what you are going to do next. It might be something you have already done and enjoyed, or something else you want to try.

Sleep is for superheroes!

Sometimes going to bed can feel like the last thing you want to do — there is so much fun to be had when you are awake. But sleep is so important for your body. Without sleep, you would not have the energy to do all the things you love.

When you sleep, your brain is still working. It processes everything that has happened in the day, cleans away what is not needed, moves things you have learned from short-term to long-term memory and works on solving problems. If you did not sleep, those things would not get done. Having a good night's sleep also helps you concentrate and remember things more easily.

What to do if you wake up during the night

- Even if you do not want to get out of bed, get up and have a wee as that might be what woke you up.

- Keep the lights off, as bright light will wake you up more.

- Lie back down and take deep breaths. Breathe in counting to 5 and out counting to 7.

- Try not to look at the time, as this might make you worry about how much (or little) of the night is left. Instead, think about how comfortable your bed is. Imagine floating on a cloud.

- Work through your body from your fingers to your head and down to your toes, trying to relax every muscle. See the progressive muscle relaxation on the opposite page.

"Sleep is the single most effective thing we can do to reset our brain and body health each day."
– Matthew Walker

Sometimes getting to sleep can be hard, but there are things that can help.

- Moving more during the day.
- Being outside in daylight as much as possible.
- Having some calm time in the lead up to bedtime.
- Writing a list of what you need to do the next day.
- Writing in a journal about how you are feeling.
- Progressive muscle relaxation. Lie down and work through your body from your toes upwards. Clench each part for a few seconds and then relax it.

For a few days, make a note of what you did during the day and before bed, how well you slept and how you felt. Try some of the things above and see what helps you sleep better.

What I did today	What I did before bed	What time I went to sleep	What time I woke up	How well I slept/ How I felt in the morning

Claiming your space

You do not have to do anything out of the ordinary to claim your space, you just need to be yourself. For you, claiming your space might mean doing something extraordinary. Find inspiration from these people who have had the courage to be themselves or taken a stand for what they believe in.

NO.

Rosa Parks was told that she had to give up her seat on a bus so that a white person could sit down. Being black was part of who she was, and she knew that it did not make her any less important than anyone else.

Jaden Smith does not let gender stereotypes restrict what he wants to wear. Nor does he let anyone's idea of what a boy or man should look like stop him from wearing skirts. He has said that he hopes that by doing this, it will make it easier for others to break out of gender stereotypes.

Greta Thunberg knew that something urgent had to be done about climate change. She was fed up that nobody was taking action, so she organised a strike at her school. This one small step started a global movement of school strikes, even though everyone told her she was too young to make a difference.

Lizzo is a black American pop star who celebrates the skin she is in and the person she wants to be. She challenges stereotypes and expectations about what a woman is expected to look like.

Everybody grows at different paces and there are many different ways that people can feel about how their body will change as they get older. Some people may just be overwhelmed by how their body will change, while others may feel that their gender identity does not match the one they were assigned at birth. If you are worried about going through puberty and the effects it could have on your body, a good first step is to talk to someone you trust about your feelings.